A Salesperson's Guide to a Successful Life….and Career

Copyright © 2009 by James R. Wallen All rights reserved

Contents

Acknowledgements

These acknowledgements are somewhat different than other publications, primarily because the content is based on personal experience and the sharing of stories with fellow salespeople. I haven't copied from other books or from surfing the net. Although when it comes to methodology, I am happy to point you to the companies I believe currently provide the most valuable training.

In chronological order: (last names have been left out to protect the guilty).

I need to first thank my father who taught me there isn't a gray area; there is only black and white. When it comes down to it, you know if you are doing the right things for the right reasons.

My Mother who taught me that family, friends and love should always be high on your priority list.

Eddie, who owned the first car dealership I worked for, taught me how to be hungry, fearless and aggressive. I still think the best training you can give a new salesperson is putting them out on the point of a car dealership for a few months. This will teach or remind them of the hard-core basics of sales.

Janice who gave me the opportunity to meet with and learn from hundreds of CEO's as a kid just out of college.

Kelly who was the first CEO I worked directly for, taught me how important it is to be passionate about what it is you sell and what your company does.

Sue, whom as a Regional Director, taught me the importance of the "details," and follow-through.

Denton, Michael, John, Kenny, Jeff and Orlin from whom I learned that starting a company and selling a product are very different animals, and how important friendship and teamwork are in sales.

SV who gave me the opportunity to sell 7-8 figure deals, taught me so much about business and technology, tested me in almost every way, and as a result I became a stronger person for living through it.

Bob, the best boss that anyone could ever hope for and whom many salespeople follow wherever he goes. From him I learned the many great traits that make an amazing VP of Sales. Whenever I am forced into management roles, I pull from that experience consistently.

Overview

To start with, thank you for taking the time to read this book. The reason I am writing is pretty simple. Flying back from a trade show in New York, I was thinking about all of the sales professionals I had caught up with and how they were doing.

For the most part they fit into the mold of the high-end salesperson: well compensated (but don't save much), under-appreciated, out of shape, travel a lot, dress well, golf well, have more than their fair share of vices, usually a few marriages and kids from different wives, and also have at least a touch of something most people would call charisma. They are fun to be around and usually their employers see that as what their job really entails.

Other than being well compensated, dressing well when I have to and having a touch of charisma, I would say I do not fit the mold. I would also say it took a lot of effort over my career to push back against that mold. When I look at my colleagues, I can remember a time when they pushed back as well. They are still fun to be around and at least put forth to the public that they are successful and happy. They do this while their finances; marriages, pipeline and families suffer.

Portions of this book may seem to be common sense and there were pieces that I was undecided about leaving in. However, after reviewing the book myself, I realized that there were times in my career where I wish I had taken my own advice. All salespeople have found themselves working in an environment for a company or selling a product that is totally dysfunctional. We ask ourselves, "How in the hell did I get myself in this situation?" There are warning signs before we take the job or developing while we are there. Salespeople tend to be looking more for immediate gratification, so we overlook discrepancies, don't ask the questions that we don't want to know the answers to, quit our jobs and go were we hope the grass will be greener. I hope this book serves as a guide so you do not find yourself in this situation.

This is not a sales process book that will get pushed on you during your orientation by your employer or manager (Although I believe following a defined methodology is a key to success and suggest some in the book). The reason this is so, and the reason why this is distributed in a "viral" way, is that in many cases your employer, manager or company product may be a huge roadblock to your personal success and happiness.

This is also not a best practices manual for sales. At a previous employer, we had a consultant come in for a 2-day sales skills session. He made sure we knew to brush our teeth, give a firm handshake and try not to stare at a female client's breasts. The majority of what he covered was so basic that the person who had chosen the training company was "reassigned" to a different business unit. If you are looking for common sense tips like this or "how to get past the gatekeeper" this is not the correct book for you either.

I hope to take you down a path that forces your employer, manager and product group to treat you differently, or find themselves without salespeople. In the end, I believe the real change this will force will be positive for everyone: companies, managers and products. We can take off their blinders and they can pull their heads out of the sand, as we are truly their eyes and ears to the market.

However, many companies will resist changing the way they operate and the way they treat their salespeople. I want you to be able to identify these companies quickly for a simple reason; so that you go to work for someone else, or better yet, don't start working there in the first place. This book is for you, "the salesperson," and not the company or the manager. That is why you won't receive this book as part of a training or orientation. That is why you should let your fellow salespeople know about it!

Who is the author? I have sold everything from eight figure software deals to fortune 500 companies, to outsourced services, to cars at the local dealership. I have been successful with regards to making money, and more importantly growing a marriage and family, which I look forward to being part of every single day. Most importantly, I can't imagine being happier.

I think it would be most productive if I leave out any more details for one reason. If I told you I was 65 years old and had hit my quota every quarter for the last 40 years selling steak knives, 80% of you would say I have no idea what it is like selling what you sell, and to whom you sell it to. If I told you I was 35 and retired selling software and basically had a handful of huge deals, 80% of you would say that I have no idea what it is like selling what you sell, and to whom you sell it to. At the end of the day, no matter what I say, 80% of you would respond with, "You don't understand my situation; it's different and I'm special." Don't we hate it when our prospects say that exact same thing?

With that said, I agree with you. You are special and you need to work for the right company, selling the products that best fit you.

If you are happy with your life, make enough money, spend enough time with your family, enjoy your work, love the way you work with your boss, truly believe in your product, rarely get angry or stressed about work, then do not waste any more of your time reading this!

Chapter 1- The Right Product

I can't count the number of times I have heard people say, "You can sell ice cubes to Eskimos," or "Bubble gum to the lockjaw ward," etc. Bottom line is the guy who sells ice cubes and has been given a territory populated with Eskimos, isn't going to have ongoing success. The salesperson who sells bubble gum and is wasting their time pitching folks in the lockjaw ward is an idiot.

Products fit into roughly 3 different categories: Commodity, Value-Add, or Premium.

- A Commodity only sells based on price. In order to provide the cheapest product, the company must have the most efficient forms of production and distribution.

- Value-Add products produce additional value based on added supporting services and functionality, which differentiates the product from the competition. They sell based on ROI and Total Cost of Ownership. They maintain an account management function that supports customers after the initial purchase.

- Premium products are recognized based on quality, performance and brand. The product and support are the absolute best and therefore companies can charge a premium for it.

A great exercise is to look at all of the U.S. companies that have filed for bankruptcy in the last year. You will find the majority sold a Commodity, a minority sold a Value-Add, and hardly ever did a Premium product company go out of business. We will explore this in more detail in the next chapter as well as discuss how to choose the right company for you. However, you need to open your eyes when you choose a company to work for. Ask yourself, "How will what you're selling affect your day-to-day life?"

What will affect you more directly is the price point of the product you are selling. Not to make things any more confusing than they need to be, but products fit into 3 price categories: Transactional, Functional and Budgetary.

- Transactional are lower amounts; decisions can be made from a single contact and can be made by any person. Most transactional purchases are made by a consumer, not a business.

- Functional purchases are for "proven" products that are usually a requirement of doing business, but are at a higher price point. Depending on the price point, these purchases can sometimes be made outside of a budgeting cycle, but are usually made by committee.

- Products that fit in the Budgetary price point are what we traditionally identify as a "complex" sales cycle. It usually takes at least a year, requiring executive sponsors, Requests for Information, Requests for Proposals, decisions made by a committee, and finally negotiations handled by procurement and lawyers.

The first puzzle to solve is "which product you are going to be most successful selling?" It's common sense that the bigger more expensive products will make you more money than the smaller ones, or is it?

Let's take high-end software for starters. An Enterprise Application that helps a business run more efficiently can cost in excess of seven million dollars in software and services. A qualified sales executive makes a base salary north of $120,000. Their commission on the sale might be around 2% of the sale, so in the end, that rep can sell one deal in a year and make $260,000.

For a Functional purchase example we can use high-end hardware (computer servers). In this case there has already been a business decision that is driving the need to buy a stack of servers, making the servers a requirement of doing business. A qualified sales executive in this arena makes a base salary north of $100,000. Their commission on the sale might be around 2% of the sale. At $6,000 per commission check, this rep must get a lot more deals than the salesperson that handles Budgetary purchases.

Finally, there is the Transactional purchase that covers anything from magazines to copy paper to cars. A qualified salesperson here might have a base salary anywhere in the range of zero to $80,000. The consummate salesperson can actually make a lot of money here, but will always be working the angles, and is making and answering calls on his/her cell phone 14 hours a day.

Looking at the options, everyone says they obviously want to sell the most expensive products for a premium company. That may very well be the case for you, but there are several other items to consider.

The first is the number of variables under your control, and the second is the total market available. Both of them go hand-in-hand. The larger the price tag, the smaller the target market is that can afford and/or has the need for your product. The larger the price tag, the more variables there are out of your control.

If you sell a Transactional Commodity, it is a simple numbers game. You make X number of calls, you get Y number of appointments; those appointments convert X percentage of the time into orders. A great sales person can vary the conversion rates slightly from appointments to deals, but come W-2 time, the most important variable is how many calls they made. Sounds horrible to some, but consider the fact that almost everything is within your control. You are truly the master of your own destiny and every day you decide how much money you are going to earn for the year, based on your effort. If you make your numbers, you pretty much are left alone. It doesn't take much time to get to know your product and industry. You can climb the ladder of seniority easily as most others will burn out quickly for lack of challenge and laziness. The downsides are that your earnings are fairly capped and limited, you will not feel challenged, and the managers of these environments tend to micro-manage.

Let's take a look at a Functional, Value-Add environment. This product has usually been around awhile and the space has several competitors. Thus the driver to create value-added services is to differentiate. Territories are usually well defined and demand for the product is usually forecasted to a degree of certainty. You will find the sales professionals in these companies have been around awhile and will have "cherry picked" the best territories. The procurement process is definitely longer than a transactional sale, but shorter than a budgetary sale. The buyers have a good understanding of who the players are and what the general offering is.

To win the deal you have to do much more than have the best price. You have to have the best product knowledge and thorough sales process to sell to all stakeholders in the prospect. You will have plenty to challenge you: a never-ending amount of analyst coverage to monitor and competitor information to stay on top of but you will also have a territory that has real potential, a career path with a company that is probably stable, support from the product side of the company, a matching 401k, etc.

The downside is this sale usually requires a hefty team effort. You depend on product and services support to win deals, and some of your destiny is out of your hands. If you are the guy who says, "There is no *I* in team, but there is one in *profit!*" you probably won't be very happy here. There is a high degree of office politics as folks who have been around a long time position themselves against each other for career advancement. Although this is more complex than a Transactional product, there is some pressure on price, so the margins are still not gigantic, and one deal does not usually make your year. This environment attracts managers that are very detail-focused, which is why they were probably successful in their careers. They will be all over you for details, reports and administrative, life sucking, bureaucratic red-tape crap. Hopefully I didn't let any slip there about my preference. The bottom line: if you aren't a team player and if you don't have attention to detail, this isn't a good fit for you.

Finally we talk about the Budgetary sale. This is the traditional complex sale for which you will find thousands of books written by folks who were lucky enough to be involved in a big deal. The reason there are so many books about it, is straight forward. It's just fun to be a part of a big deal. You sell to people who are higher up in organizations, it requires C-Level sign off, you deal with big numbers, everyone in the company roots for you, the pay day is huge and if you have a couple deals under your belt you become James Bond. You have a license to do whatever you want. Your CRM reports aren't up to date, neither are your expenses, you don't even pretend to fill out time sheets and Human Resources has been told to stay out of your way. It is what I call an evangelical sale. You must be extremely passionate about your product and what it does for the customer, and you have to have the ability to spread that enthusiasm to the prospect.

The downsides are as disappointing as the upsides are exciting. The sales cycles are extremely long. If the company tells you that the sales cycle is 9-12 months, that translates into a reality that your commission is probably 2 years out from the first call. Within these companies there is usually a continuous battle for recognition and after you close a deal, everyone in the company will claim that they were ultimately responsible for the deal. "What have you done for me lately?" is the attitude for all salespeople. With such long sales cycles, the company feels bitter writing a commission check after paying your base salary for 2 years. The targets are always too few and all your eggs are in one or two baskets. There are many variables that are out of your control, which is extremely frustrating with only a couple real deals brewing. One company will declare bankruptcy while your deal is tied up in legal, and the second deal will go to a competitor because they gave the CEO stock under the table. That leaves you with no deals for the year and a whole crew of Monday morning quarterbacks questioning how you weren't on top of the account and managing the process.

The best fit for this product is someone who can work with a large team and bring in the right people at the right time, document and follow a process, have no need for recognition outside of your commission check, have patience and above all be very passionate about your product.

So just as a summary, if you have a problem with details, being a team player, have little patience, or require company recognition then you need to work on these aspects or find more of a transactional product. If you are looking for an longer career with a company, are detail oriented, don't mind a lot of paperwork, enjoy continuous education about product and market, then more of a functional product will be an area where you can excel. If you have patience and can "quarterback" a large team, then you can try a budgetary product.

Be forewarned, the days of just taking customers golfing and drinking are over. While you will depend on subject matter experts at different points in the sales cycle, companies now expect you to take the prospect 80% of the way there before leaning on the team. Overlay positions in pre-sales and inside sales are now shared across a greater number of salespeople. To earn the confidence and support of the company, you can't bring them into every meeting and you have to generate leads for yourself.

Your last task is a bit of research. All companies go through product evolution. The product starts as something new and exciting and more of an evangelical sell with a budgetary purchase. Then competition enters the market, white papers and ROI become documented and the sell moves to a Functional product. Companies run out of ways to create a value add and the product becomes a Commodity. Finally a new product hits the market that renders your product obsolete.

Know where your product is in the cycle and how long it will be there before you make your decision as to where you will succeed. Plan ahead and look at the direction your company is currently heading and make a decision as to how long you should stay.

Most importantly out of everything in this section, remember this: *"Don't sell ice cubes to Eskimos, sell them hot chocolate."*

2.   The Right Company

It is rare that the CEO of a company came up through the sales organization, and there are obvious reasons for it. Traditionally the powers that be in a company are highly educated, visionary, very structured, organized and great at delegation. I would be the last one to make the argument that these are not extremely valuable traits. However, they are usually complimentary to a bureaucratic, work-aholic and egotistical personality. CEO's have sacrificed a lot for the pursuit of success and many times missed out on social opportunities, leaving "people" skills lacking. They see their sales force as a necessary evil and pricey cost center. In the CEO's mind, a salesperson is golfing, smoozing, pounding the pavement, and focusing on the relationships that enable the more valued assets to get in front of the customer.

Unfortunately this general attitude filters down through the organization and salespeople don't get the focus or support from services and product groups. These companies are usually easy to identify and spend more time trying to create ways *not to pay* their salespeople, as opposed to finding ways to attract, keep, compensate and motivate the best people.

This section helps you identify the type of companies that value their sales forces. This analysis is best done before you decide to work for a business. If that is not possible and you are committed to your current employer, then you are faced with the task of altering the current culture. Obviously it is easier to identify a company that values sales, as opposed to changing the mindset of a company that currently does not, so let's start there.

Companies usually do press releases when they are hire a new CFO or SVP of Product Development. Check to see if the company did a press release when they hired their previous Head of Sales. Second, check the press releases of major new customer acquisitions. Is the Head of Sales quoted in the release, or is the communication from other management positions? Third, look on the company's website page which introduces the management team. Is the Head of Sales mentioned, and if so, toward the bottom or the top? These are all small things that shed light on the company culture and how they view the importance of sales.

It may seem silly, but you should also ask about the company's travel and expense policies. If 50% of the time salespeople are expected to be on the road, but must take the cheapest flight regardless of the number of connections, stay at cheap hotels and eat cheap food based on a per diem, that says everything you need to know about how much the company values sales.

In one company the CEO had read an article about how the largest mass merchant in the world had its employees double up in hotel rooms to save money. They did this at all levels of the company, which created a culture of understanding about the importance of keeping costs down. The CEO had all of us bunking up when we traveled together or when we attended trade shows. I personally spent many a night doubled up in a hotel with that particular CEO, and I must say that I got to know him better than I ever expected I would get to know my boss.

This is an area where you have to do your homework. When a company hires an executive, they go through massive search and background checks. As professionals, we need to do as much due diligence as the company does. Ask the company these tough questions:

- Who was my predecessor?
- How long was he/she in the position?
- Why did he/she leave?

After getting this information, finish with the ph test question for B.S. - "Is it okay if I contact my predecessor?" This question merely tests their reaction, because you should contact them regardless of how they answer. If they give you the contact information or not, you can still search them out.

There is a small chance when you find them that they tell you exactly what the hiring company told you, and you are inspired with hope that this is the "perfect job." They tell you they moved up through the ranks, hit quota for 10 years and are retiring to spend more time outside and less time traveling. They also say you are inheriting a full pipeline and the market is far from penetrated. Okay, that little fantasy is over. What they do tell you should be taken with a grain of salt. In reality, it's more likely that they don't have that job anymore because they either found a better one, their boss was horrible (see next chapter), or they failed.

Another way to gain insight as to how a company views sales is to find out the total sales organization turnover figures. If you look in the Want Ads under Sales, you will find that some car dealerships are always hiring sales staff. They churn and burn through them. This is the extreme and dealing with more of a commodity, you would expect this.

As part of the interview process, when they ask to check references, be prepared with your list of references. My previous employer requested 10 references, including 2 people I had sold to, 2 people who had worked for me and 2 people who I had worked for and 4 personal references. The CEO called and spoke with all 10.

The mistake I made at the time was not asking him for 10 references. I should have asked for a few personal references of my CEO, a few references from employees who had left the company, a few customers, their lenders, etc. It is unlikely that they want you to contact customers, but you should speak with several current sales reps, pre-sales, inside sales, marketing and administrative staff.

In high-end jobs it is common that they ask to see previous years W-2's to verify how successful you have been in the past. You should be prepared to do this; however, you should also ask them to see a cross section of W-2's from their existing sales force if they do. They obviously can't show you employees W-2's, but they can take the names off the W-2's and give sample data.

By asking if you can speak to the sales support groups, you will learn several things. Do they have pre-sales, inside sales, marketing or administrative staff? If they do not, this is either an early stage company, a company that doesn't understand the value of sales (i.e., they compensate their sales people to operate on an island), or they are a company doomed to fail in sales.

The questions to ask the current sales staff should be objective and purposeful. A few examples might be:

- How long have you worked here?
- What are the strengths/weaknesses of the company?
- Have you made quota the last few years?
- What have your earnings been?

- What are the biggest challenges to hitting your numbers personally?
- Why did the person who had this position before leave?

These questions will provide valuable insight into whether the position is really the job you want. If this is a territory that is a stronghold for the competition and the last 5 salespeople have failed, do you really want it? I understand your ego may tell you that you are an amazing salesperson and you can succeed where everyone else failed. Wake up, your common sense will tell you to find something else. You will also find there is a discrepancy between what the company says the sales cycle is and what the sales reps say it is. Ask yourself "How big is the discrepancy?" and "What else is the company being misleading about?"

One of the most important conversations is about compensation. Most companies give you a range and then put off further discussions until much later. You can tell a lot about a company based simply on the amount they pay in base salary vs. "at plan" commissions. Key questions about the compensation plan may be:

- If an early stage company, are they offering equity?
- If they are giving equity, in what form are they giving the equity?
- How long is it before the equity vests?
- Does it automatically vest upon change in ownership?
- What percentage does the equity really calculate to?
- Do they have a draw, and if so, is it recoverable?
- What are the benefits?

The questions above are really a starting point. You may discover other questions of interest to you based on the different types of compensation plans you've worked under in the past.

Another important component to find out is how and when commissions are paid? If commissions are paid when the customer pays, you need to plan on that accordingly. In enterprise software for example, you may be told that the sales cycle is 12-14 months. That probably means 12-14 months from the time they are looking at a project to the beginning of a "pilot." They then will pay a portion of the services for configuration of the pilot, which takes 3-6 months, and then want the pilot to be in production for 3-6 months. They will evaluate the results from the pilot and make requests for changes prior to a complete rollout. Those changes are made, delivered to the customer for acceptance, there is testing and then they will probably want to re-negotiate the numbers on the Enterprise License. It then gets sent back to legal, and you are able to send them an invoice, which is net 30-45 days before they pay. Congratulations!! It's now more than 2 years later and you receive your commission payment. If the space is a bit more mature, and the company values sales, they will probably do something such as pay 50% of the commission upon initial contract signing.

On one end you have a company that views sales basically as a manufacturers rep role and on the other you have a company that views sales as an important component of the organization. This isn't a dig against manufacturers reps. I know several that are very successful. They are paid 100% on commission and are able to represent several different products and companies. The have no company-paid benefits, but they are their own bosses and have spread the risk across several providers for whom they sell.

When it comes to compensation and sales, there is one question you absolutely must find out.

"What percentage of the existing sales force hit their quota over the last few years?"

I love when a company tells you that your "at plan" is $375,000 and that is all they say. Then they tell you that your base is $25,000 and you ask them how many salespeople hit their "at plan," - to which the answer is always zero. What you are looking for here is the opportunity for continuous success. You are looking for a company that creates stretch goals, which are attainable and not continuously adjusted. You don't want a company that reacts to a salesperson hitting their number by always increasing the quota.

When you dig into how the company came up with the "at plan" number of $375,000, their thought process is always comical. It usually goes something like this: The CEO says based on his business plan that he wants to grow the company to $20 million in revenue this year, 3 of the 4 sales people have quit or been fired, and the company is filling one of the positions - so the end result is a sales staff of 2 people. To hit the number the CEO pulled out of his backside, each salesperson must do $10 million in sales and close 3 new deals. This must be accomplished even though it is already the 3rd quarter, the pipeline for the year is really already set, and you haven't even been hired yet much less ramped up. If you are a salesperson you probably find this somewhat amusing. If you are or have ever been the Head of Sales, please be careful getting back into your chair after the fall, take a moment to compose yourself, and catch your breath from the laughter.

I am biting my tongue to not name a specific tech company, but it is a great example. This company hired a friend of mine and told him he would be given a couple large opportunities for new business and a crowd of existing customers to maintain, or slightly grow. If you crack one of the big prospects, you bank huge commissions for the next 6-8 years off that one deal. If after a couple years you do not crack one of the few big opportunities, you will probably move on, whether it is by your choice or by the company's. As I expected, he cracked one of the opportunities with a very large shoe company based in the northwest. What I didn't expect was his employer's reaction, which was to promptly take the account away from him and assign it to a "more seasoned" Account Manager. This is behavior coming from a large technology company, which traditionally has a reputation of treating its salespeople well. So you can imagine what can happen in a company that has a reputation of taking advantage of its salespeople.

Another example is a startup company I previously worked for. At the end of the first year they gave a bonus to all employees based on their performance evaluation. We were new to the market and no one expected us to close any deals the first year. The pipeline was full and the second year was set to be a good one. My performance evaluation was outstanding in all areas. Yet, I was informed by the CEO that the first year bonus applied to everyone in the company except me. In this company the message was clear. As a salesperson you are truly evaluated based on one thing and one thing only; that is your revenue production. I am not saying there is anything wrong with that, as long as you understand that is the case and are comfortable with your ability to achieve specifically what they want – "Results!"

In the interest of reciprocity you should then prioritize your work and reports back to your employer in a similar manner. If an employer treats it's salespeople like hired guns, then they should expect them to act like hired guns. This employer should then:

- Expect to get very little feedback from the market about the product fed back to the product group;
- Expect reports to be filled out when it is convenient for salespeople;
- Expect salespeople to refuse to travel on weekends, refuse to work late nights, never share best practices with other salespeople; and above all,
- Expect them to ignore the non-compete that won't stand up in court, and go to work for the competition when he/she is FED UP!

I had the privilege of being in a meeting where the new CEO of a Fortune 500 Company was introducing himself to his employees. This is a company that had almost no turnover. If you had a job there you were guaranteed a job for life and your kids could probably count on one as well. The CEO started his introduction by explaining what he called the "New Contract." He said employees were guaranteed a job as long as the company didn't have a method for doing it cheaper, faster or better. His message was clear. If you wanted to keep your job you had better make sure you were the best, fastest and most cost effective option.

This "New Contract" has been the approach that many companies have taken in the new world economy. There is nothing wrong with this philosophy, as long as you are aware of it. You should also understand that a contract, whether it is new or old, goes both directions. If the stance of your company is along the lines of the so-called "New Contract" then there again should be reciprocity. You will commit to working for and selling a company's products as long as there isn't a company that will pay you more or provide more opportunity than your existing employer.

Spend time with key people from other parts of the organization and make sure you are surrounding yourself with an "A" team. If the company values sales, they should be setting some of these meetings up as part of the interview process. Are you meeting with the services group, product group, support group, finance group, etc? If you are not, then the company does not place value in sales. If you are, then you need to spend as much time interviewing them as they are interviewing you.

Plan ahead and know the questions you want to ask to really help you evaluate the company and the executives you are meeting with. Ask the product group what the future roadmap looks like, and what the key differentiators are in the product. Ask the services and support groups what the biggest challenges are with product. Ask the finance group about the long-term goals of the company: to go public, to be acquired, etc.?

The last variable you should investigate is the variable most salespeople spend little to no time on at all and it is usually to their detriment. That is **"Is the company positioned to succeed?"** It will make no difference if you hit your quota if no one else does, and services are unable to deliver anything you sold. If a public company, there is more financial information available than you will ever need, but at the very least you should review the balance sheet. How much runway does this company have? If a private company, then request basic financial information. What are the company's quarterly revenues for the last 8 quarters; and what are the expenses, liabilities and assets? If you hear the term, "runway," too much you should be skeptical. Companies that continually focus on cash flow, getting additional financing and runway, tend to focus more on "not losing" than on "winning." My experience is these are the companies that struggle. If they do succeed, it takes too long. Usually much longer than your average, immediate gratification-motivated salesperson can stand.

The key message here is reciprocity and due diligence.

- Do your homework and find out how the company truly operates.
- Ask the questions that will help you determine culturally how they feel about and treat their salespeople.
- Don't take anything for granted.
- Plan ahead!
- Be true to yourself - be only as loyal and committed to your company as your company is to you……..

3.   The Right Boss

Every salesperson has horror stories about bosses and cry the motto, "Those who can't sell...manage." If I focused on these stories and bad managers, I'm afraid it would take up volumes of space with no productive outcome. However, the fact is the vast majority of people quit their jobs as a result of their direct report. Your happiness depends so much on your relationship with your boss whether he/she is a Director, VP or CEO. To succeed, it is imperative the relationship be healthy and productive. Making it even more complicated is the fact that the average lifespan of a VP of Sales within a company has gotten shorter and shorter.

This section helps you identify your best style of being managed - *it may not be what you think* - and also helps to identify whether a company develops good managers. Good managers treat their people differently depending on the needs of each salesperson.

As salespeople we have a tendency to group managers into generic boxes such as micro-managers, hands-off managers or bureaucrats. We often do this for selfish reasons. A micro-manager knows where you are and what you are doing at all times. A hands-off manager leaves you alone and views a good percentage of their job as "shielding" you from executives - so you have the time to sell. A bureaucrat is concerned with politics and reports for their own career advancement. Make them look like a hero and nothing else matters. These categories are probably too general to provide value, which is ironic as that is what salespeople should be concerned with. **Does your manager or will your future manager provide value?** Let's start with a quick story to kick off the conversation that you should have with yourself.

My favorite manager had the philosophy of taking the time to find the absolute best salesperson for the job, investing the time and resources to give them everything they need to sell, and then staying the hell out of their way. He made sure you felt you could call on him as needed, while also making sure the company resources were at your disposal. He was hired as VP of Sales to manage the salespeople directly, which previously was done by the CEO. This manager lasted only a few months before he could no longer "shield" his salespeople from the CEO.

During the 5 years I was with this company, we cycled through 12 salespeople, all of whom where professional and successful in previous endeavors. Not a single salesperson stayed as long as 2 years - actually most left before their first year anniversary. All of them left as a result of personal differences with the CEO. Reporting to the CEO, there were times when I was tested and broke my personal rule that if you go home more than 2 days in a row miserable and it bleeds into your personal life, you should put in your 2 week notice.

This was a time where I reported directly to managers that were polar opposites in their management style. The question that I ask myself is why I stayed after my favorite charismatic VP left, when I was again faced with dealing with the challenging CEO. I answered my own question - he was *challenging,* which was exciting to me! He tested me on a daily basis to become a better salesperson. I was continuously given opportunities to grow that I had never had. Information was always shared with me that was for my personal benefit.

Granted, the CEO was abrasive and intimidating and there wasn't anyone who ever stood up to him. Yet, I realized early on that it was a difference in communication styles and not a personal assault. It was okay to push back as long as you had your reasons, they were rational, and you were willing to defend them. During my time working for him I believe I was the most challenged, most aggravated and also the most productive. When I look back and try to dissect the experience and determine how I survived when no others did, it narrows down to what is important. First he altered his management style over time as my abilities and strengths changed. For the first 6 months he was by my side in every detail. As I became more capable and his comfort level increased, he gave me more room. Second, I learned from him every day, as he provided *value* and perspective that I did not have. Finally, looking back on the experience, I realized I actually liked the guy!

I admit I have become a bit cocky and tend to expect more from employers as I have developed in my career. What I would love to have in an ideal world is:

- A company and product that I have taken the time to determine that success is absolutely achievable;
- To work with my boss to determine stretch, but achievable goals for the year;
- To receive the necessary training to be able to intelligently sell the product;
- To know where to turn in the company for needed support;
- And finally to be able to call my boss at the end of the year to schedule my congratulations dinner, President's Club gift, Diamond Circle Vacation, etc.

Lovely, now let's return from la la land. We have to let go of that defense mechanism that says, "Those who can't sell...manage." This is a negative knee-jerk reaction to a boss that merely wants to help us. Regardless of the horror stories you have about your past sales managers, you should pretend the scent of turkey and mashed potatoes is filling your nostrils, and be thankful for what you have.

Imagine being an engineer in a field where the best engineers are also managers of other engineers. I have seen it first hand and as I am sure you can imagine, great engineers do not usually make great managers. The most productive thing when evaluating your best type of manager is to put yourself in their shoes for a brief period of time. In general, they usually have good basic selling skills, have some history of success and experience, and now have entered management. Their success now rests on your shoulders. So let's take a look at what they have to do, what information they need to know, and why.

In reality, a company must be able to forecast revenue by quarter, get market feedback as to the product direction, manage the bench in services based on expected demand, and make adjustments to company operations based on cost of delivery of the product. Which means that across all of the salespeople the company should have a comfort level with everything in the pipeline, with confidence of close and projected close dates. There needs to be a systematic way of capturing feature/function requests from the market and feeding that information into the product group - *Sales are the eyes and ears of any good company.* Whether your company has larger services or production/manufacturing components, they need to accurately forecast resource requirements to manage their costs and profitability. All of this leads to the immutable truth – *Yes, you will have to do reports and paperwork.*

The biggest struggle I have is that not only are reports and paperwork part of the job, so is teamwork at varying levels. It is easy for most salespeople to share their best practices with other team members because they enjoy showing the depths of their knowledge. However, getting that person to take constructive criticism from their boss is when the pressure in the vault of the sales ego starts to build. If your current or future boss had significant success in the past, it can result in 1 of 2 things. It could be that they want you to do everything as they did; hence, you have little control over your sales strategy and you are miserable. Or, it results in an environment where you can learn new and successful strategies, be challenged, and augment your stockpile of skills.

Find the boss that provides value in the form of suggestions and ideas around strategic planning whom you can learn from. Stay away from the boss who wants everyone to do exactly as he or she says without discussion or debate. The boss that you have to be wary of is the wolf in sheep clothing. They do a great job at pretending to listen to you and brainstorm, making you feel like you have had your input, but in the end they get you to do things exactly as they wish. After all, they were at one point, salespeople and understand that people support what they help create. Make sure that they don't follow the practice of people support what <u>they think</u> they help create.

What you should look for in your boss is a manager that questions the value of any and all requests on a salespersons time that take away from selling. Be cautious of micromanagement here. A manager should find efficiencies in administrative tasks and eliminate redundancies.

In regards to administrative type tasks, you only need to look so far as the regular sales meetings to measure the value the sales administration brings to you. If there is a weekly scheduled meeting on your calendar; that is, not in and of itself, a bad thing. But heed caution if you find the following:

- There is no agenda ahead of time sent to the attendees.
- The meetings are often cancelled moments before they are supposed to begin.
- The Head of Sales is the facilitator of every call, and talks more than 50% of the time.
- It is rare other departments take part in the call.
- There is little interaction between salespeople.
- You find you can mute your phone, put it on speaker and take your morning shower without anyone noticing.

Poor management is a <u>lack of value placed on the salespersons time</u>. Let me show you what I mean. Poor managers:

- Say the focus is to have you out in the field, but then spend 2 hours telling you why it is important for you to do so.
- State and restate the same bullet points over and over again in a different way.
- Call every day to "brainstorm" because they value your opinion, but do not give you a chance to voice your opinion, only to ask you what is new and exciting for the day (which means daily update).

What is hard to understand is that these types of managers do not consider themselves micromanagers merely because they don't ask you daily for an update of how many calls you made, to whom, how many messages you left, how many live conversations you had, how many resulted in scheduled web meetings, and how many resulted in scheduling live meetings. That is not micromanagement; it's more like breastfeeding an 11 year-old. It's really not right and you know you should say something, but not sure if it's your place to do so. If you find yourself in a position where you are being managed in such a fashion, the company you work for is either trying to get you to quit to avoid paying unemployment, or they truly are ignorant. Either way you should find another job immediately. Don't worry about leaving on good terms!

Another tendency of a poor manager is to make something a standard operating procedure with very limited data points as proof of causal relationship. Let me give you an example. Take an athlete who had a great game on the day he put on dirty underwear and who was shut down the night before by his girlfriend. He then, makes the assumption that wearing dirty underwear for every game and abstaining from sexual relations will guarantee a future of "WINS!" To make matters worse, this is not a player; he is the team manager. This manager then decides to make every player on the team wear dirty underwear and chastity belts. Can you imagine?

More realistic examples might look like this:

- You start a campaign with new messaging to your total market of 400 potential customers. You get some feedback from one prospect, which causes the executives to want to change the total campaign based on that 1 data point.

- You pick up the phone to cold call a
  couple customers before an upcoming
  conference; because you don't have the
  traction you need coming out of inside
  sales. On your first call you schedule
  an important appointment, so the
  executives make you Head of Inside
  Sales.

There are hundreds of examples similar to the ones
above. My point is to keep a look out for managers
that have a knee jerk reaction to every data point.

This is also a simple symptom of excessive pressure.
Pressure from the CEO, The Board of Trustees,
and/or The Shareholders, rolls downhill, and almost
always lands on sales. The more pressure there is,
the more the sales organization looks like an escape
artist underwater having a difficult time getting the
lock picked. The frantic look in the eyes as oxygen is
running out results in continuous tweaking of
everything, even before the process has been given a
chance to produce results. This general tire spinning
creates chaos, discontinuity and general waste.

The bureaucrat and the hands-off manager often feel
the same. The only difference is their motivation. A
bureaucrat wants you to be left alone and wants to
serve as a pass through for communication. This is
so that they can take the credit, or pass off the blame.
They include other departments in sales meetings
when they have the opportunity to impress, and when
the quality of these presentations and obvious time
investment is head and shoulders above any effort
that has been put into a customer facing presentation.

On the flip side is a manager that views their job as
"shielding" you from executives. If you find a
manager who feels their job is to limit access of their
bosses, their days are numbered. Don't walk away

from this boss and job… RUN! The hands-off manager often times reports back to the executives the current status of events and pipeline, without asking the folks in the field. Best-case scenario, they want to "shield" you from administrative tasks. Worst case, it could be because they are worn down and beat up by the CEO, they no longer care about their jobs, they are looking for their next gig and they merely want to say whatever it takes to drag things out until they find their next opportunity.

The micromanager is the introvert that is focused on too much of the detail and shouldn't have gotten into sales in the first place. The bureaucrat always looks and acts the part, but would stab you in the back without hesitation to insure their place in line on the career ladder. Finally, the hands-off manager is the cool guy that acts like your buddy, but is probably doomed to fail. Great list to choose from isn't it? So which manager is the best manager for you? That is something I can't answer for you. You must do the work and figure out the manager that best fits your style and needs.

To do this you must be honest in identifying your own strengths/weaknesses and your long-term goals. For instance, I tend to not focus enough on the details, so I need a manager who is a bit more of a micromanager. At the same time, I can't and won't tolerate a short leash. Depending on the company I may or may not have aspirations of jumping up a few notches on the corporate ladder. If my boss is a bit bureaucratic and I have confidence they will actually climb the corporate ladder, I may not be opposed to taking their vacated position. However, I have a problem with accepting a job that requires more hours and responsibility with less pay, so if that is the case, I could care less about my boss's career aspirations. I have plenty of friends, so I don't need my boss to be yet another, so if he happens to be abrasive then that is fine as well. I have gone through the exercise of sketching out what "my perfect boss" would look like, and I am in a better spot for it. I would suggest you do the same!

However, I have missed the single criteria that should guide all your thoughts with respect to the person you report to. **Can you learn from this person?** Just like any confident salesperson, it is difficult to admit you don't know everything. It is hard to admit there may be a different way to get in the account, to identify the key players, to win them over to your side, to negotiate the deal, etc. I had bosses that were literally so incompetent I would not trust them to walk my dog. They lacked leadership skills, did not inspire passion, were unorganized, didn't respect my time, had zero presence in front of customers, and worst of all, did nothing to help close deals. I had no respect for them, and **respect** is what is most important. Spend some time with your "to be" new boss before you take a job. Determine if you will respect them, learn from them, and if they will provide value. If the answer is "No" to any of the above, you will not be happy.

As a final note, it doesn't matter how much time and effort you spend on identifying the perfect boss, because odds are they won't be there for long. Do a bit of homework to find out how long they may be there before changing companies or careers to follow a mentor. If a company burns through a CEO or VP of Sales every year, then you know what you should do.

I actually wanted to follow a mentor to a new company where he became Head of Sales. They flew me out to meet with all of the company executives. I told my mentor the only reason I wanted the job was because he was my "perfect boss." He knew there were a lot of politics in play at that time. Although it would have been good for him to hire me, he told me I shouldn't take the job, as he probably wouldn't be around for long. The definition of Protégé is roughly "one who is protected." My mentor did his duty to me as his Protégé.

In summary, you have to put yourself in your boss's shoes, get to know them and their motivations. When they are under pressure, and they will be, how will they react? Is this someone you can learn from? Do you respect them? Will they lead? Will you follow?

4.   Your Time

"If you can't sell, drive like hell" is a quote primarily directed towards those who drive in a territory and receive a mileage reimbursement. The problem with this approach is that your margin on cost of gas, maintenance and depreciation of your vehicle over your reimbursement does not come close to justifying the time you spend in your car. It also points to the strategy usually employed when a sales group is having trouble hitting its numbers. **Spinning your wheels as fast as possible to create the illusion of movement is my biggest pet peeve.**

Time is your most valuable commodity. While we all have heard we should work smarter not harder, we rarely execute on this, and we tend to work for people and companies that would prefer we do both.

When it comes to working smarter, you need to invest some time in a methodology and hone your skills. There are many resources I can suggest you turn to in order to do so (Miller Heiman, TopLine Leadership, Dale Carnegie to name a few). As a professional, you probably have already gone through a half a dozen of these trainings so I won't spend much time on methodology here. I will however, say that most salespeople don't follow a methodology even though they have been through several trainings. Go back and review and put together a game plan for your activities. That is what makes you a professional. If you don't, then picking the right job won't be your biggest challenge; it will be finding someone who will employ you.

This section helps you avoid companies that place little to no value on your personal life. It will also provide the tools you need to keep the rest of your life in balance. I want to give you the tools you need to prioritize all of the elements of your life, including family, hobbies, health, religion, community and education, in order to fit them all in and still have a successful career. You have to answer the question, "Do I live to work, or do I work to live."

If you work to live, then start with a simple exercise. Put together a time budget. It amazes me how many people have never actually looked at where they spend their time. We know exactly where our money goes, but have no idea where our time went. You can always find ways to make more money, but there is no way to make more time. You have to make the most with the time you have.

Start with the time you spend at work. I actually work for a company where I fill out a time sheet and allocate where I spend my time each week. Can you believe that? Now consider that I fill it out the same way every week and I just write in that I spent the week prospecting, doing customer meetings and follow-up. This is an example of a waste of time that serves no purpose. Sorry, had to get that jab in.

There are some basics that are common sense here. I have a friend who lives in Fort Collins, CO. and landed his dream job in the tech center on the south side of Denver, CO. However his dream wife didn't want to leave her dream town of Fort Collins so he commuted every day 90 minutes each way. That is 3 hours a day spent in the car, 240 days a year. If you worked there for only 10 years, you would spend 7,200 hours driving in your car. I thought this was crazy until I started selling to companies in the North East and New York. I found it was common that professionals commuted by train to Manhattan from at least 90 minutes away. I guess they are at least on a train and many of them work on their laptops or read the paper. They may also be catching up on phone calls while their bluetooth headsets suck their brains out, and they speak louder than necessary to insure others are forced to listen to their conversations.

To look at this line item called "commute," you don't have to be in that obvious of a situation. I worked for a company that had offices downtown and I lived about 25 minutes away. For most that is a very reasonable commute. Now take into account how long it takes to pack up your laptop, get gas for your car, find a parking space, pay $15 a day, walk to the office, boot your computer, pack up your laptop at the end of the day walk back to the car, get stuck in unexpected traffic on the way home, etc. This 25 minute one way commute quickly turns into 70 minutes a day of unproductive, stress time.

My primary job at this company was selling expensive software, and guess what? There wasn't a single person in my office that was in the market for multi-million dollar software, so there really was no reason to traipse into the office every day. Salespeople spend enough time in airports, waiting in security lines, checking out rental cars, checking into hotels, waiting in corporate lobbies, etc. Don't waste more time commuting than is necessary. If you are the VP of Sales it may be more necessary to be accessible and part of the day-to-day operations; however, if you are actually doing the selling, it is not. Working from home is a privilege though, and if abused, can be lost. If you work from home it is even more important to conduct a time audit.

The commute is just one of the line items you should have in your audit. The other line items will vary greatly, so the best way to start is to capture everything you do in a week. You will find items that naturally cluster into larger categories. It is important that you are honest with yourself. Don't ignore anything you spend time on, even if you might be embarrassed by it.

I found I would start off every day surfing the Internet for relevant topics to my industry and prospects. I would often get pulled off topic and waste time reading information that was irrelevant. So I started using clipping services to surf the net for me and just send me relevant articles.

You can look at categories that were obvious the first week, such as "meetings," and further break them down into "external meetings, internal meetings, valuable meetings and waste of my time meetings." Obviously the next step is to find ways to avoid getting sucked into the meetings that are a waste of time. Or, you can provide feedback in such a way that the meeting becomes more valuable to you and the company.

There are other obvious areas you can work on. The areas that show themselves as significant wastes of time are areas such as chatting in the break room, smoke breaks, long lunches, checking personal messages, etc. While some of these are good for social status within the company and keeping up on the informal things, I guarantee that you could and should cut some time out here.

For some of the big chunks of time, it's essential to stay on top of technology and best practices in order to cut them out. If you travel a lot for work, make it a goal to do twice as many meetings over the web and fewer face-to-face. While your "old school" boss that traveled with an overhead projector and transparencies back in the day will struggle with this, your CFO will shower you with laurels if you hit the same or higher numbers with significantly reduced travel expenses. The argument your boss will make is that you can't build those personal relationships without being face-to-face all of the time. Taking the client out golfing and drinking is the "old way" of sales and there is a smaller and smaller place for it in today's market.

I have never known of a deal of any significant size that was won because the company truly liked their sales guy better than the other sales guy. One caveat; I have seen deals that were lost because they disliked the salesperson, or because the lack of professionalism proved to be something the customer didn't want to sign up for in a long term business relationship. At the end of the day, a personal visit from just the salesperson does little to further your opportunity, so don't waste so much time on it. Visit a company in person when they are qualified, and then do it with a Splash! Bring in subject matter experts and services folks to build credibility in your offering, and bring in a strong executive to build confidence in the roadmap and vision of the company.

If it is time to hit the road, shuffle through airports, breath recycled air, loose your luggage, deal with delayed and cancelled flights, rent cars, get lost on the way to meetings, and eat horrible food, at least use your time well.

- Purchase an extended battery for your laptop and work on the plane (do you really have anything better to do?)
- Obtain priority or elite status with an airline, car rental brand and hotel; and negotiate with your employer to use those companies even if there is a reasonable difference in cost.
- Work out at the hotel gym every night or morning, and eat decent food at good restaurants.
- Use a web cam or similar technology to Skype the family every night.

- Above all, please get to the airport early and plan on arriving at your destination with plenty of time before your meetings start.

I look at business travelers who are always cutting it to the last minute to get on the plane for every flight. You can tell they are going to have a heart attack before they are 45 years old. There are so many ways to travel more efficiently without dramatically increasing your blood pressure. When the FAA changed their policies about carrying liquids on planes, a huge number of passengers began to check their luggage. I felt sorry for my female counterparts who had no chance of getting all their hair products into a ziplock sandwich bag, while I chose to shave my head bald. Seriously, if you add 10 minutes to check in a bag and 10 minutes at luggage claim and you travel 30 times a year, that is 10 hours sucked away from you that you will never get back.

How many trips have we taken where we got in front of the prospect by telling them we were already going to be in town with another client and wanted to see if they had time to catch up - when actually didn't have another meeting scheduled. Have these meetings ever proven to be valuable? Why do we continue to set them up? It's because we don't have enough activity showing up on our weekly or monthly reports, so we in turn spin our wheels to create the illusion of movement.

The next big chunk of time to eliminate is with the same prospect that has been on the pipeline report for the last 4 years. They reach out to us at least once a year to kick the tires. In truth it's a bored Project Manager who actually does a pretty good job of staying educated on several different areas. This is so they can maintain a reputation of being knowledgeable, while actually never spearheading any projects. Better yet, it is a company with a reputation for bringing in solution providers that are on the cutting edge, learning everything they can from them, and then building something themselves.

We must get better at qualifying out prospects. Opportunities need to be moving in some direction at all times. If what you sell, "Didn't make the budget this year," that's fine. Find out why it didn't make the budget, what types of projects beat yours for budget and do better next year. Move it to the maintenance category and move on.

For the example of the company that has a reputation for wasting vendor time and building it themselves, don't ever let them get in your pipeline. Don't even return their calls. There are several companies I simply refuse to call on. One of them is always an executive dream and they want to be able to say that they landed this giant company as a customer. You need to let them know up front that it's not worth your time and you don't have an interest in selling to them. Give the prospect to someone who wants to work for several years to win a deal that will ultimately loose money, but in return be a great kudos for your company. The commission on kudos is usually pretty slim. Another company is a fairly small player that I have had success selling to before. Even though they are a small player, they act like the biggest fish in the pond and make it painful, laborious and long to sell to. The commission check on these smaller deals isn't worth the pain.

We have all heard of the 80/20 rule, and it goes for time as well. You will spend 80% of your time on the deals that will make you 20% of your money. You will spend 20% of your time on the deals that will make you 80% of your money. The key is to allocate your time appropriately. My favorite old western story is of a bank robber that kept getting caught and thrown in jail. When he was asked why he keeps robbing banks he responded, "That's where the money is!" As a sales person we need to have the same philosophy, only do a better job at staying out of jail. Take your time audit and allocate your time proportionately to where your money will come from.

The next thing that needs allocation is pretty simple; it's called the rest of your life. If I were to calculate the things I value in order of importance to me, it would look something like this:

- Family
- Friends
- Activities (Skiing, Rock Climbing, Mountain Biking, Karate, etc.)
- Health - both physical and spiritual
- Community
- Career
- Life-long learning and growth

The dilemma is clear, without a successful career, I can't afford the best for my family, can't take part in activities, can't give back - at least monetarily - to the community, etc. So career needs to be much higher on the list, perhaps even the top. However, when you do a time audit you should look out for what ends up, for most salespeople, looking something like this:

- Career   85%
- Family   3%
- Friends   1%
- Activities   1%
- Health   2%
- Community   0%
- Learning and Growth   0%
- Have no idea   8%

The above is roughly how I used to spend my time. You may be saying to yourselves that this is awful and you are really a better father/mother husband/wife than that. But take a look at the numbers and find out if you really are. Did you spend more than 4 hours of **real quality** time with your family last week? If not, then your numbers may not really be any better than these.

The key changes I made were eliminating the 8% wasted time that I didn't know what I did with, working more efficiently and effectively so I could get more done in fewer hours, combining time with family and friends, activities, health, community and learning so that it looked something more like this:

- Career   50%
- Family   20%
- Friends   15%
- Activities   10%
- Community   5%
- Learning and Growth   5%

As a final step you need to set parameters and make difficult decisions. I used to have a rule that if I didn't get in 30 days of skiing and 30 days of rock climbing then I would put in my 2 week notice immediately. Those parameters have changed as my family has grown and my priorities have shifted. After setting those parameters, discuss them with your direct report. When everyone is on the same page, everyone is much happier. Finally, when you need to make those difficult decisions about priorities, try to occasionally make them in favor of simply what makes you happy. I have several friends, one a CFO and another a partner in a large law firm who continually choose work over all else. They try to schedule in fun, but work always trumps a ski day. It has been years since I have skied with Rich or Andy!!!

WORK TO LIVE, DON'T LIVE TO WORK!!!

5. The Choice

"ABC-Always be Closing", "Coffee is for Closers" - There are many quotes around closing. My hope is you don't work for an organization that still tries to identify the "closers". The view that closing the deal is some magical thing that happens with a wink, a forked tongue that hypnotizes customers to spend money and seals the deal with a handshake is ludicrous.

Selling is a process with several effective methodologies. The salesperson that wins the deal is usually the one who is in the right place at the right time, follows a methodology, sells a good product, has good product knowledge and support from their company, and who ultimately follows through. I will not completely discount that magical quality called charisma. It is subjective and impossible to quantify or track. There are traits in any person that other people find themselves drawn to.

This section helps you make the choices that lead you to be a person others are drawn to. It also improves your chances of being with the right people at the right place and time to close the deal. It ties all of the other sections together.

In my experience, happiness is to a great degree a choice, as well as a self-fulfilling prophecy. I once dated a girl that became upset when I didn't spend all of my free time with her. I was in college, starting a student organization, loved sports, and had friends I liked to spend time with as well. When I did spend time with her, she constantly griped about not getting to spend time together. In no way did that make me want to spend more time with her. It was a self-fulfilling prophecy.

I have found the same to be true with sales. People like to be around other people who are generally happy. Not to the point where they are constantly laughing at nothing in particular and reciting songs from "Annie" while rock climbing (which I have been know to do). People are generally drawn to others who are successful, confident, and pleasant to be around. However, if you stumble in your career or loose a few deals, your happiness and confidence suffer. Your prospects will be less inclined to spend time with you, you won't understand their needs as individuals as well as your competition, and you will loose the deal. You become less happy, which carries over into the way you walk, talk and hold yourself.

We all know a person who seems somewhat aloof and too carefree. Everything always seems to work out for them and things come easy. Most people respond to this person with angst and disbelief. We say, "They have no idea what it is like, I have to work twice as hard for everything." While we gripe and moan, we don't understand why it is hard for us to schedule meetings and why people don't want to go out of their way to be around us.

When I was in college, I worked for a car dealership when there were a few months where sales were down, and it just seemed to snowball. Now customers are already dreading the moment when a car salesman walks up to them to start the process, multiply that by 10 when the salesperson is having a bad month, which all of us were. The General Manager gave out several spiffs on a Saturday, which is obviously the busiest day of the week. He gave out $50 to each salesperson who could get a family jumping up and down in the bed of a pickup truck, $75 for each family that a salesperson could convince to have one of their kids get in the trunk of the car and actually close it, and $100 for every customer that didn't want to take a test drive that you could get in the back seat of a car, engage the child-proof locks and drive off the lot. This quickly turned into mass chaos, pandemonium, and also the most fun I have ever had on the job. The net result was that all of the salespeople immediately loosened up, they were having fun, customers were more approachable, and soon we were busy doing paper work and putting temporary tags on cars!

Obviously in a more complex sales process this is an exaggerated exercise that wouldn't work. The idea is the same, get your work done but make the choice to be happy, have fun and be optimistic.

Charisma is similar to the quality of leadership. I recently googled "leadership and it came back with 243 million results, while charisma came back with only 10 million. If you get into the subjective discussion of what makes a good leader or a bad leader, you can have endless discussion. That does not change that a leader is simply someone who is followed. Martin Luther King Jr. was a leader, and so was Adolf Hitler. It would be a pretty simple debate as to the qualities of each, but nonetheless people followed both.

Charisma is simply a trait that most leaders have and in it's most simple form can be defined as a magnetic personality. People are attracted to other people of all different shapes, colors, sizes and personalities. As a sales person, knowing this puts you ahead of most others. Some people are attracted to people who talk a lot and others are attracted to people who are more reserved and good listeners. Someone who is charismatic, I believe has the ability to be both, depending on who they are working with. I think you know where I am going with this and could give you dozens of examples of different traits that people enjoy at opposite ends of the spectrum. You need to be able to adapt to your environment and the people that you are with and the first step is to be perceptive. Look for what makes others happy and comfortable, by putting others ahead of yourself, you will finish first!!!

Wake up every morning and make the choice to be happy, do the work that actually moves opportunities, make the choice to work out and be healthier, make the choice to plan out and spend quality time with your family, make the choice get out and get involved in a new hobby and cut an hour of TV out a day, make the choice to learn and continually make yourself better, take the risks in life that you only get once in a while, choose a company to work for that will be successful and support your choices!!!